Things You Can Do to
LIVE A
JESUS-CENTERED
LIFE

H. R. CURTIS

CONCORDIA PUBLISHING HOUSE • SAINT LOUIS

1   2   3   4   5   6   7   8   9   10   22   21   20   19   18   17   16   15   14   13

TABLE OF CONTENTS

And a ruler asked [Jesus], "Good Teacher,
what must I do to inherit eternal life?" Luke 18:18

Along the way, I am sure at least one teacher
told you that there is no such thing as a stupid question. But
this question from the ruler to Jesus is something worse: it is
nonsensical. What can I *do* to inherit? That just doesn't com-
pute. What can you do to inherit Bill Gates's fortune? What
can you do to inherit the English throne? Try as you might,
work as hard as you could, there is nothing you could ever
do to inherit these things. That's not how inheriting works.
Inheriting is not dependent on what you do but on who you
are—or better yet, on whose you are. Are you a child of Bill
Gates? Then you get the fortune. Are you the son of the
queen? Then the throne is yours. You didn't ask for it, you
didn't earn it, but it is yours.

Salvation is like that. You can't earn it. It's not dependent on what you do. It's an inheritance. You get salvation
because of whose you are: you are God's child, a member
of His family. He bought you fair and square with the life of
His Son, Jesus Christ. He adopted you into the family through
Holy Baptism. He has declared you to be a son or daughter,
and that's that.

So then, why is this book called *5 Things You Can Do to
Live a Jesus-Centered Life*? It's a good question. We do want
to avoid the ruler's mistake: our salvation, our life in Christ,

is not based on our actions. But there is more than one mistake out there. For every way that is right, there are at least two ways that are wrong. Two and two make four—if you say "three" you are wrong, and if you say "five" you are wrong. The ruler was wrong in thinking that he could earn eternal life. And we Christians would be wrong to think that what we do in this life does not matter and has no bearing on our life of faith.

Again, think of the example of an inheritance, either a fortune or a throne. Fortunes can be frittered away and lost. Or they can be used for frivolous spending. Likewise, once you become a monarch, will you rule wisely or poorly? Will you abdicate the throne and throw it all away? Paul talked about how this applies to our Christian life in 1 Corinthians:

> For we are God's fellow workers. You are God's field, God's building. According to the grace of God given to me, like a skilled master builder I laid a foundation, and someone else is building upon it. Let each one take care how he builds upon it. For no one can lay a foundation other than that which is laid, which is Jesus Christ. Now if anyone builds on the foundation with gold, silver, precious stones, wood, hay, straw— each one's work will become manifest, for the Day will disclose it, because it will be revealed by fire, and the fire will test what sort of work each one has done. If the work that anyone has built on the

foundation survives, he will receive a reward.
If anyone's work is burned up, he will suffer loss,
though he himself will be saved, but only as
through fire. (3:9–15)

The foundation is set: it is Jesus Christ and He alone. Your salvation is secure. How will you now build on that foundation? With wood and hay or with silver and gold? This is why so much of the New Testament Epistles is filled with encouragements for holy living. The apostles did not want their hearers being "saved, but only as through fire," by the skin of their teeth. They wanted their hearers to live Christian lives full of the joys (and the crosses) that come with a life of service toward God and neighbor.

This book is about living a full, vibrant, joyful Christian life in the midst of a fallen world. It is about the necessary bearing of the crosses that Jesus said would come our way if we wanted to be His disciples. By the grace and power of God, *you can do it*.

If you are going to live a Jesus-centered life, you had better start by getting Jesus. And we meet Jesus where He wants to be found. While we can certainly appreciate the glory of God in the created world—the power of ocean surf, the majesty of the mountains, the infinite expanse of the stars—nature can only take us so far. God has made us no promises in nature. No matter how closely you paid attention to the world around you, you would never learn who Jesus is and what He has done for you. In short, the world around us can teach some things about God—His power, holiness, justice, and so on—but none of these deals directly with our salvation. God's salvation promises come to us in very specific ways because He has made us very specific promises.

The theological term for these specific promises is *the Means of Grace*—the ways that God has promised to bring us grace, life, and salvation. Here's a short listing of those promises:

WORD: "Jesus said . . . , 'If you abide in My word, you are truly My disciples, and you will know the truth, and the truth will set you free' " (John 8:31–32).

BAPTISM: "Repent and be baptized every one of you in the name of Jesus Christ for the forgiveness of your sins, and you will receive the gift of the Holy Spirit" (Acts 2:38).

ABSOLUTION: "Jesus said to [the apostles] again, 'Peace be with you. As the Father has sent Me, even so I am sending you.' And when He had said this, He breathed on them and said to them, 'Receive the Holy Spirit. If you forgive the sins of anyone, they are forgiven them; if you withhold forgiveness from anyone, it is withheld' " (John 20:21–23).

THE LORD'S SUPPER: "Now as they were eating, Jesus took bread, and after blessing it broke it and gave it to the disciples, and said, 'Take, eat; this is My body.' And He took a cup, and when He had given thanks He gave it to them, saying, 'Drink of it, all of you, for this is My blood of the covenant, which is poured out for many for the forgiveness of sins' " (Matthew 26:26–28).

These are God's specific promises regarding the delivery of salvation. You don't have to wonder where you can find God and His grace; He's already told you the answers. You will find God in His Word, Baptism, Absolution, and the Lord's Supper. And, of course, all of these things come together in the church.

Now, you probably don't need a book to learn that you ought to go to church in order to lead a Jesus-centered life. But I hope that the rest of this chapter will teach you how to get more out of church each Divine Service—and even challenge you to see that there is more to church and these

Means of Grace that you may have been missing up to this point in your Christian life. Furthermore, the future chapters will tie in to this chapter on going to church, tying the whole Jesus-centered life together like spokes connecting to the hub of a wheel. If we want a Jesus-centered life all week long, then it is vital that we get Sunday morning right and live our Jesus-centered life from the altar of Jesus outward.

Make Time

Human life is nothing more and nothing less than a collection of time—and a finite, limited collection at that. So what you do with your time indicates your values and priorities. An hour spent watching sitcoms, an afternoon driving back and forth running errands, a lunch break working out at the gym, or an evening out with your friends speaks volumes about who you are.

When I first began my ministry, I received some excellent advice from a more experienced pastor. He told me to keep a journal of everything I was doing every fifteen minutes of every day for a week. The idea comes from the "billable hours" diary that lawyers and other professionals have to keep. They have to be precisely and specifically accountable for their time. The diary I kept that week taught me a lot about how I was conducting my ministry, and it's an exercise I've returned to many times to evaluate how I budget my time.

To attend church and a Bible class each week will take about two hours of your time—maybe a little more depending on how far of a drive you have. Take a moment to think through your week. How many activities in your week take up more than two hours of your time? How many of those activities are absolute necessities (eating, sleeping, working) and how many are optional and at your discretion (TV, reading, working out, talking on the phone, surfing the Web, kids' sporting activities, etc.)?

If you want to live a full, vibrant, joyful Christian life there is simply no substitute for weekly attendance in church. It all begins there at the Means of Grace place, where all of God's specific promises of salvation are given out. This is the hub of the wheel. The rest of the Jesus-centered life connects to this hub. Take away the hub and the wheel doesn't work—start skipping Sundays and see your Christian life unravel.

So make the time. Make the reception of God's Means of Grace your priority. This will likely mean sacrifices for you. The world does not respect Sunday as it used to. There are sporting events, work requirements, and so forth that can conflict with Sunday attendance. These conflicts generally fall into two categories: hard and soft conflicts.

The hard conflicts. We'd all like to have jobs where we could always have Sunday off. But we can't all have that. Some people are employed as shift workers in local manufacturing. One week they work the day shift, the next week afternoons, and the next weeknights. Others work four days on, four days off year-round. Their employers may not differentiate between the days of the week. My father worked for years in the grocery business—there are no weekends off, because people shop on weekends.

So how do we make time in the face of such hard conflicts? It is that question that has led some congregations to start a midweek Divine Service specifically with shift workers and those who have to travel for work on weekends in mind. If these hard conflicts are an issue for you and your church attendance, talk it over with your pastor right away. There is simply no substitute for weekly attendance in the Divine Service.

The soft conflicts. A child's sports team, vacations, a tough week at work and a desire to sleep in on Sunday— setting any of these things aside to make time for church is a real sacrifice, but it's a sacrifice that pays off in the long run. After all, what is more important to teach our children: teamwork on the field or God's Word and putting Him first in our lives?

Getting Something Out of Church

But church is so _____ —you fill in the blank: *boring, slow, early, tedious, loooong.*

My wife feels the same way about the movies I like, but to me they zip by. Likewise, I can't make it through many of the books she can't put down. I don't understand what she sees in them, and vice versa. If she could understand what it is I like about French spy movies and I could understand what she likes about nineteenth-century English novels, I'm sure we would have fewer disagreements about how to spend our evenings. But when it comes to entertainment, some stuff just isn't for some people.

However, church is not entertainment. Church is for everyone. God's Means of Grace are meant for all His children. If you learn the rhyme and reason behind what we do in church, it will make sense, and you will get more out of Sunday morning. Even if you have loved church your whole life, you can dig deeper to learn exactly why it is you love it and how you can express that love of church to others.

The church service itself is a drama—not a made-up drama like a play or a TV show, but a real-life drama taking place in the chancel and in the pews each and every Sunday, a drama in which you have been called by the Holy Spirit to play a role.

If simply making the time to be in church every Sunday is the first and indispensible step in living a vibrant Jesus-centered life, then seeing and understanding what Jesus is doing with you each Sunday in the Divine Service is the next step. So let us now walk through the Divine Service, learning your role in the drama of Sunday morning.

Finding Your Place on Sunday

God is everywhere. But a God who is everywhere can sometimes be hard to tell apart from a God who is nowhere.

The incarnation of Jesus, the coming of God in the flesh to Bethlehem, is God's proof that He is not just everywhere, He is *here*. The Divine Service is about the continuing here-ness of Jesus. In the Divine Service, we are in the real presence of God. For by His gracious invitation, we are called to the Lord's altar to receive Him in His body and blood. Jesus is really there. He really is. This is the point of departure for the entire Divine Service: the bodily and bloody presence of Christ. How should I comport myself in His presence? How shall I prepare to receive Him? How shall I honor Him? These are the questions the Divine Service is answering.

First, like Isaiah, you proclaim your unworthiness in a general Confession. Before we even dare to set foot in that area of the church (the chancel) where Christ will make His presence available for us, we plead our unworthiness and beg forgiveness. We are coming into the presence of God, and that causes sinners to shake in their boots (Peter: "Depart from me, for I am a sinful man, O Lord" [Luke 5:8]). But we know that God is merciful in Christ and desires to forgive us ("If we confess our sins, He is faithful and just to forgive . . ." [1 John 1:9])

Then, having confessed our sin and begged forgiveness, we hear Christ's word of Absolution spoken in the voice of the pastor, announcing that we are indeed forgiven through the mercy of God delivered in the salvation work of our Lord Jesus. Absolved, what do we do now? We are here to receive the Lord in His body and blood, to be in His presence—how shall we prepare? We pray. But how shall we pray? What better way than to use the prayers God Himself gave us: the Psalms? So as we enter the chancel in the person of the pastor, we chant the Introit, a collection of psalm verses that sum up the theme of the day. God has given us His Word, and we have nothing better to say than His own Word back to Him.

After the Introit, we are in the chancel, in that sacred space where our Lord makes His presence available to us in His Sacrament. It is awe-inspiring and mysterious to be here. So once again we plead the Lord's mercy in the Kyrie: Lord have mercy!

Notice how movement is key to the Divine Service. We are constantly moving up toward the chancel, toward the altar, toward the climax of the service in the Lord's Supper. We show this in our architecture: the altar is centered and on a higher plane than the rest of the sanctuary. Other Christian traditions won't have a centrally placed altar precisely because they don't believe in the real presence of Christ in the Sacrament. But for us, there is a growing sense of anticipation as the service literally moves closer in time and space to the living presence of Christ.

As we draw nearer to Christ in the Divine Service, we sing a song of His presence, the Gloria in Excelsis, the song of the angels when Christ first made known His bodily presence among us at Bethlehem. Each Sunday is not only an Easter, but a Christmas as well. Jesus rose on Sunday, so it is Easter, and He was born in the flesh on Christmas, so each Sunday at the altar is Christmas for us as we receive Jesus in His true body and true blood in the Sacrament.

Having praised the Holy Trinity for His salvation, we are ready to again approach Him in prayer—this time a prayer for the things we desire, a prayer not strictly taken out of the Scriptures like a psalm verse but a prayer that is a collection of the desires of the people: the Collect. But who would dare to approach God in prayer on behalf of the people of God? Only a man called by God through His Church to do it. And so the pastor asks for a blessing from the people—a reaffirmation of his ordination. But how else could there be to ask a blessing in the church except by giving one: "The Lord be with you"? Then the people bless him in response: "And with thy spirit" (*LSB*, p. 189). And only then, with your blessing, does the pastor pray.

So we have confessed, prayed God's Word, asked His mercy, received and asked His blessing, and prayed that our own desires might conform to His holy will. How shall we know God's will for us unless we hear Him? So the reading of His Word comes next—from the prophecies of Christ in the Old Testament, to the exhortations of the apostles in the Epistles, to the voice of Jesus Himself in the Gospel.

Having heard the words of Christ in the Gospel, we respond by speaking back to Him what has been spoken to us. He has told us who He is, so we confess in the Creed that we believe His Word.

Now we have climbed quite high. We started on the floor level, confessing our sins and begging mercy. We then climbed toward that place made sacred by the Lord's presence and cried for His mercy again. We have prayed, praised, and given thanks; we have heard God's bracing Word of life in the midst of death, which surrounds us, and we have confessed that we believe it. The journey to the altar thus far has been like climbing Everest at a brisk pace. We need a way station on the path to the summit of the altar. We need time to reflect on the Word of God that we have heard—to slow down and mark, learn, and inwardly digest this Word so that we can be prepared to receive our Lord. But like the Ethiopian in Acts 8:38, we must wonder, "How can I [understand], unless someone guides me?" And so the Lord gave Philip to that Ethiopian, and He has given churches men called and ordained to preach His Word.

The simplest thing you can do to get more out of the pastor's sermon is to listen. Jesus tells us the preaching done in His name is supposed to be about "repentance and forgiveness of sins" (Luke 24:47). In Lutheran terms, we call this Law and Gospel. The Law shows us our sins, where we need to repent. The Gospel shows us the forgiveness of sins won for us by Christ. Listen for those specific things in the sermon. How is the pastor trying to show you your sins so that you evaluate them and repent of them? How is the pastor showing you Jesus and how He takes your sins away? How is the pastor showing you the new life you live in Jesus now that you are forgiven?

After the sermon we prepare to resume our journey toward the altar and the reception of our Lord in His Sacrament. First, the gifts must be gathered. Our Lord instituted His Supper so as to be bodily and bloodily present in, with, and under the bread and wine. Where do this bread and wine come from? From the Lord blessing His people, of course, from their generous tithes and offerings back to the Lord. These are brought forward in the offering: the sweat of their brows, their bread of death scratched from the thorn-infested ground (Genesis 3:19). But behold! What comes up as bread from the people, the sweat of their brows, the bread of death, will be returned to them as a blessing. The Lord takes this sign of the curse and returns to us a blessing: the Bread of Life who has come to save us from our sins.

The wine, which the Lord made to gladden the hearts of men and lighten their toil, will now be, by the power of Christ's Word, the choicest wine of heaven, His blood, the new testament poured out for the forgiveness of sins.

Can you see how even what seems the most mundane thing in the service, the gathering of the money, is actually connected to the altar of Jesus, that is the self-giving of Jesus? Our stewardship is a response to God's grace, but more than that, our stewardship is transformed by God's Word into a blessing. Part of going to church is this sacrificial giving that God then uses to continue to bless us with His Word and Sacrament. Again, the words of Jesus say it best: "Where your treasure is, there your heart will be also" (Matthew 6:21).

Your heart goes where you "invest" what God has entrusted to you.

But back to the drama of the Divine Service. The altar is now prepared, the bread and wine are laid before the Lord. Now we again ask the Lord's blessing in prayer—prayers for the Church (the whole people of God gathered in Christ's name) and prayers for all people according to their need (1 Timothy 2:1–4), as we prepare to receive the One who died for all people. These are the prayers of the Church. It is both our duty and our privilege to bring our petitions before God. This is the congregation's prayer, and all are invited to add their voices to each petition, responding with "Hear my prayer" or with the words from the Kyrie, "Lord, have mercy."

The Service of the Word, the great preparation for the Supper, is now ended. We are ready to head out from base camp and make the final journey upward to the summit—it is time for the final push—it is time for the mystery of salvation—time for the servants of Christ to "do this in remembrance" of Christ as He commanded. Again: who is worthy? Who would dare speak Christ's words to bread and wine and expect His body and blood to be there also? Only a man called to do so by the Lord through His Bride, the Church—and so again, the giving and receiving of the blessing is enacted, the pastor's ordination renewed: "The Lord be with you." "And with thy spirit." From the oldest liturgies we possess, these words of the general preface are here, calling the people to lift up their hearts and hands to the Lord that He might change and renew them. It is right to give thanks to the Lord. Truly it is good, right, and salutary to praise and thank God.

What is a fitting eucharist, a fitting thanksgiving? Our minds are once again filled with thoughts of Isaiah brought before the altar of God—we are nearing the presence of the Lord, the very definition of heaven. Well, then, let us sing the song of heaven coming to earth: "Holy, holy, holy is the **LORD** of hosts; the whole earth is full of His glory!" (6:3). But now, what is this? The next words are not from Isaiah in the temple but from the crowds on Palm Sunday: "Hosanna to the Son of David! Blessed is He who comes in the name of the Lord! Hosanna in the highest!" (Matthew 21:9).

Heaven has met earth! The seraphim are in the same company as the smelly, teeming crowds of Jerusalem's narrow streets. The Word is made flesh. The highest God is also the man on the donkey. And that Word incarnate is coming to us, the same God in that same flesh and blood hidden in, with, and under the bread and wine where only the eyes of the faithful can see.

This is our thanksgiving—completed now in that most eucharistic of prayers: the one He gave us. "Hallowed be Thy name": that is what we are here to do, let it be done in us! "Thy kingdom come": the kingdom of God is among us when Christ is with us. "Thy will be done on earth as it is in heaven": we are here to do His last will and testament, to "do this in remembrance" of Him, to have heaven on earth. "Give us this day our daily bread": oh yes, this bread of death—make it our daily Bread of Life! "Forgive us our trespasses": for You instituted this for the forgiveness of sins! "Lead us not into temptation but deliver us from evil": nothing could guard us from these things like Your own holy body and precious blood.

Do you begin to see what is missed if the Divine Service is seen as just a random collection of holy-sounding words? There is a story here, and it is not a story concerned just with the ancient past. You are not only in it, you are really living it right now! You are the one who has been called by the most holy God to receive the benefits and blessings He has worked for you. You are the one who needs to bless the pastor for his work so that he can pray for you, preach to you, and serve you the Lord's gifts. You are the one who is drawn up into the salvation story by singing the angels' song and the song of the Palm Sunday crowds. You are living out the gracious reality of God's answer to the petitions of the Lord's Prayer right there in the Divine Service.

A good introduction to the Biblical foundation of the Divine Service is *Worshiping With Angels and Archangels: An Introduction to the Divine Service* from CPH.

After the Lord's Prayer comes the words of our Lord. By the command and in the stead of his Lord Jesus Christ, the man called and ordained to fill the office of the ministry for you speaks his Lord's words, and Christian hearts believe what those words say to now be a reality. So the faithful sing and pray to the present Christ: "Lamb of God, You take away the sin of the world; have mercy on us. . . . grant us peace"

(*LSB*, p. 163). And the people of God come to the altar to receive their Lord and His forgiveness.

Then, when it is done, how shall they respond? What words should come to their lips? Uniquely, the words that come to Lutherans' lips are those of Simeon: "Lord, now You are letting Your servant depart in peace" (Luke 2:29). Simon is basically saying, "I can die a happy man! For my own eyes have seen, my own tongue has tasted, the salvation that You prepared before the face of all nations: the Christ in the flesh, the glory of Your people Israel!" We sing the death song of Simeon at the Lord's Supper so that we might approach our own deaths as easily as going to the Lord's Supper.

The summit has been reached. We've received the best heaven has to offer. After that, the service ends simply: we pray thanks for the salutary gift we have received, we are given a blessing, and we head out on our way.

That is the Divine Service, the drama of salvation with you living your role in live action. Don't you want to make time for that?

And There's More to Church . . .

While the Divine Service is certainly the center of our life in the church, there is much more to it. There are the prayer services of the church that offer scenes from the same drama as the Divine Service—praying to God, hearing His Word, having it fill our lives with its grace and power, and meditating on it through its preaching. Everything that was said above about the Service of the Word can be said about Matins, Vespers, Compline, and the other prayer services in the church. Each has its own character and blessings to bring, but chiefly, the prayer services teach us how to pray in our own private lives as well—more about that in a future chapter.

The Missing Link

Who do you think wrote the following two paragraphs?

To sum it up, we want to have nothing to do with coercion. However, if someone does not listen to or follow our preaching and its warning, we will have nothing to do with him [1 Corinthians 5:11], nor may he have any share in the Gospel. If you were a Christian, then you ought to be happy to run more than a hundred miles to Confession and not let yourself be urged to come. You should rather come and compel us to give you the opportunity. For in this matter the compulsion must be the other way around: we must act under orders, you must come into freedom. We pressure no one, but we let ourselves be pressured, just as we let people compel us to preach to administer the Sacrament.

When I urge you to go to Confession, I am doing nothing else than urging you to be a Christian. If I have brought you to the point of being a

Christian, I have thereby also brought you to Confession. For those who really desire to be true Christians, to be rid of their sins, and to have a cheerful conscience already possess the true hunger and thirst. They reach for the bread, just as Psalm 42:1 says of a hunted deer, burning in the heat with thirst, "As a deer pants for flowing streams, so pants my soul for You, O God." In other words, as a deer with anxious and trembling eagerness strains towards a fresh, flowing stream, so I yearn anxiously and tremblingly for God's Word, Absolution, the Sacrament, and so forth. See, that would be teaching right about Confession, and people could be given such a desire and love for it that they would come and run after us for it, more than we would like. (Brief Exhortation to Confession 30–35)

The man who wrote that was Martin Luther, the leader of the Reformation and the man after whom the Lutheran Church is named. He wrote those words in a Brief Exhortation to Confession, which is often appended to his Large Catechism (and is found in Appendix B of *Concordia: The Lutheran Confessions*). In the Small Catechism itself, he included Confession and Absolution as one of the Six Chief Parts of Christian teaching, smack dab in the middle of Baptism and the Lord's Supper.

In the Small Catechism, he wrote, "*What is Confession?*

Confession has two parts. First, that we confess our sins, and second, that we receive absolution, that is, forgiveness, from the pastor as from God Himself, not doubting, but firmly believing that by it our sins are forgiven before God in heaven" (p. 26).

While the absolution spoken as part of general Confession before the Divine Service absolutely delivers God's Word of forgiveness, here Luther is talking about the practice of individual Confession and Absolution. The Small Catechism says more: *"What sins should we confess?* Before God we should plead guilty of all sins, even those we are not aware of, as we do in the Lord's Prayer; but before the pastor we should confess only those sins which we know and feel in our hearts."

Does all this come as a surprise to you? It did to me when I learned of it in the midst of my ministerial studies. I didn't grow up with this individual Confession and Absolution, and maybe you didn't either. But now I cannot imagine my spiritual life without it. Obviously, Luther valued it very highly as well: just reread those two paragraphs above! There is something different, something powerful, about having the Gospel applied directly to those specific sins that weigh on you and that you find hard to shake.

This gift from God connects us to His Word, delivers us His forgiveness, and helps establish and maintain a truly pastoral relationship between sheep and their shepherds, between people and their pastors. Go to church to meet Jesus in Confession and Absolution as well. Jesus gave this authority to His ministers in John 20:21–23 for a reason—go and experience what that reason is.

Key Points

- Church is the Means of Grace place.

- There is a rhyme and reason to the order of worship.

- You have a role in the drama of the Divine Service.

- The Divine Service teaches you how to think about the things of God.

Discussion Questions

1. What did you think of church when you were a kid? How did that change as you grew up?

2. What is a sermon you really remember? Why was it memorable? Can you think of how it showed you both Law and Gospel?

3. In the liturgy we say that we are worshiping "with angels and archangels." Have you ever thought about being in church with the "whole company of heaven"? How could that insight change how you view Sunday morning?

4. Does your church use Matins or Vespers or Compline very often? Maybe for midweek Advent and Lent services? What other prayer services are used in your parish?

Action Steps

1. Make time to attend church each Sunday.

2. Prepare for worship each week with the prayers in the front of the hymnal. Use the prayers there to prepare for receiving Communion as well.

3. Listen for Law and Gospel in the sermon; take notes if you like.

4. Make an appointment with your pastor for Confession and Absolution.

I was baptized as a baby but didn't have

a terribly deep connection to the Church's life until I entered confirmation class in eighth grade. And when I did, I found the Bible to be extremely interesting and exciting: it was all new to me. But even if you approach the Bible with a new-comer's excitement and eagerness, slogging through a book like Leviticus is no easy task, especially when you come to the really confusing parts. And what happens when the newness wears off?

Jesus said, "If you abide in My word, you are truly My disciples, and you will know the truth, and the truth will set you free" (John 8:31–32). That's a great promise direct from the lips of our Lord. Setting aside time to be in the Word of God and learning how to read the Word of God with under-standing is a must for a strong Christian life. This chapter will explore just how to bring the power of the Word of God into your life in a meaningful way as part of a Jesus-centered life.

Make Time

Just as with attending Divine Service week in and week out, the first step to connecting to God's Word is making the time. If you are going to be in the Word of God daily, you have to make an intentional plan to have the time to do so.

The first advice I have here is to be realistic. If you're starting from nothing, don't say that you are going to set aside thirty minutes every day for reading the Bible. That's a laudable goal, to be sure, but nothing discourages a person faster than setting a goal and soon finding it almost impossible to keep. Whether it is a New Year's resolution to lose weight or a plan at work to start a new project—aim at a reasonable and realistic goal as a first step.

Matthew 5 is on the long side of average at 48 verses and about 1,020 words. See how long it takes you to read this chapter with good comprehension. Most adults will come in around the four-to-five-minute mark—200 to 250 words per minute. Remember, we're not trying to see how fast you can read at a dead run but how fast you can read *with good understanding.*

So, reading a chapter of the Bible plus a psalm is something you can probably accomplish in ten minutes. Therefore, as a start, try to find ten to fifteen minutes of uninterrupted time in your day to read the Word of God. Likely times include in the morning before the rest of your day starts, in the evening before bed, at a specific meal, or after the kids are dropped off at school. You have to work through your daily schedule and find what is going to work for you. The key is to intentionally set aside that ten to fifteen minutes of uninterrupted time just for Bible reading.

Breadth and Depth

There are many ways to read the Bible, just as there are many different goals in reading the Bible. We could group all of those goals into a general statement like "I want my faith strengthened through the power of God's Word." But within that general statement are a great many subcategories. Here are some examples:

- The historian who wants to trace the path of the Israelites through the desert of Sinai
- The child who wants to listen to the exciting story of David and Goliath
- The Christian who wants to know more about Jesus' miracles
- The Christian who wants to read the whole Bible
- The Christian who wants to explore a specific book of the Bible in great detail
- The pastor tracking down all of the verses about Baptism for a Sunday morning Bible class

Each of those is a laudable and legitimate goal in reading the Bible. And at various times in your life, you will change your goals. In this chapter I want to focus on the big picture: what kind of Bible reading lays the best foundation for all of those goals? As your Jesus-centered life grows and matures, you want to be able to branch out, learn more, and deepen your understanding. So you need a plan for reading and understanding the Bible that will set you up to have a firm grasp of the basic biblical message so that you can ask your own questions and have an idea of how to find answers in the Word of God.

How Can I Know?

In the last chapter, I already mentioned one of the key Bible texts for understanding how God has arranged for our life together in the Church to work: Acts 8. In that passage we meet an Ethiopian royal official. He is not given a name in the Book of Acts, but Ethiopian Christians have long referred to him as Bachos. This Bachos (or whatever his name may have been) was a Gentile—he was not a part of Israel, the sons of Abraham. Yet the Word of God had reached him and he believed in Israel's God. Like many other Gentile God-fearers, he came to Jerusalem at the time of the great feast and participated in the worship of God to whatever extent this was allowed under the Old Testament temple regulations.

But how foreign it must have all seemed! The Bible was not written in Bachos's native tongue, the worship at the temple was in Hebrew, there were so many characters in that Old Testament to keep straight, and so on. In short, Bachos was in about the same spot as you! He was a godly and pious man who wanted to know more about God and knew where to find that out: the Scriptures. But understanding the Scriptures is not always easy for us. Indeed, listen to how frustrated Bachos became:

> And there was an Ethiopian, a eunuch, a court official of Candace, queen of the Ethiopians, who was in charge of all her treasure. He had come to Jerusalem to worship and was returning, seated in his chariot, and he

was reading the prophet Isaiah. And the Spirit said to Philip, "Go over and join this chariot." So Philip ran to him and heard him reading Isaiah the prophet and asked, "Do you understand what you are reading?" And he said, "How can I, unless someone guides me?" And he invited Philip to come up and sit with him. Now the passage of the Scripture that he was reading was this: "Like a sheep He was led to the slaughter and like a lamb before its shearer is silent, so He opens not His mouth. In His humiliation justice was denied Him. Who can describe His generation? For His life is taken away from the earth." And the eunuch said to Philip, "About whom, I ask you, does the prophet say this, about himself or about someone else?" (Acts 8:27–34)

Bachos had come to the right place: the Scriptures. But he soon learned that while the Word of God is perfectly clear, that does not mean you or I are not perfectly muddled! "Who is the prophet talking about here: himself or another? I can't for the life of me figure it out!"

That's okay, because we don't read the Bible as if we were stranded on a desert island. We are not lone rangers with Bibles instead of six-shooters, rugged individuals who are capable of any feat. We are Christians who have been placed by God to be part of the Church. We stand in communities called together by the Holy Spirit through Baptism, gathered around His altar, sharing in His enlightenment, and set under the teaching authority of His ministers, for "How can I [know], unless someone guides me?"

Martin Luther's favorite term for the Holy Ministry was "the Preaching Office." The chief task of ministers is to preach the Scriptures, explain them to their parishioners, and open up the mysteries of the Bible to Christians called together as a community in that place.

So the first recommendation I have for how you can abide in Jesus' Word, be His disciple, and grasp the scriptural message is to go to your church's weekly Bible class.

Did you know that back in the sixteenth century various Lutheran state churches in Germany mandated that the sermon on Sunday morning be an hour long? Sounds like a lot—and surely it was—but the reason was simple: after several hundred years of decay in knowledge, the Church was in a sorry state. Even some pastors could not recite the Ten Commandments and the Lord's Prayer. In such a state of affairs, the only solution was to dig back into the Scriptures, and thus the mandate for an hour-long sermon.

We don't do hour-long sermons these days. Ten to twenty minutes is what you can expect for a sermon just about anywhere you go in our churches. That is enough time to preach Law and Gospel and give some insight into the Scriptures. But as a pastor who preaches week in and week out, I'm here to tell you that it's not enough time to do all that needs to be done. There is so much more packed into the psalm verses, Old Testament, New Testament, and Gospel lessons for a week that I could never unpack it in a fifteen-minute, or even a thirty-minute sermon (if folks would sit still for one of those!). To say nothing of the difficult topics that come up over the course of a year apart from the appointed readings in the lectionary.

I need more time with my flock, and my flock needs more time in the Scriptures. Sunday morning Bible class is a ready and waiting tool to solve this problem. If you are already a church-going Christian who says your daily prayers and does your best to read a little Bible every day, then there is no question what you can do to further deepen your Jesus-centered life: go to your church's Bible class.

What I enjoy most about the class I teach on Sunday morning is the ability to answer the questions that people bring with them. This gives me a chance not only to give people biblical answers to things they care about, but also to show them how to use the Bible to answer their questions. The best way to learn is by doing, and in a live Bible class you can learn how to study the Scriptures right alongside your fellow parishioners and your pastor.

Knowing the Story

Have you ever had the experience of walking up to a group of friends, co-workers, or family members in conversation and being completely puzzled by what they were saying? You understand the language they are speaking—all the words are English words and you know what they mean—but you can't place any of it in context. Finally, you ask, "What are you talking about?" And when you hear the answer, it all clicks into place.

To understand a story, you need a frame of reference for all the facts, characters, and actions you are hearing about. Understanding the Scriptures is no different. If you want to understand what God is saying in the Bible, a good place to start is by making sure you know the big picture, the overall arc of the biblical story. Then what you are reading on any one particular day can fall into place.

In this section I want to lay down that framework for you just as I would lay it down for my adult Bible class on Sunday morning.

In one sense it is easy to state the main teaching of the Scriptures: Jesus. Or as Jesus Himself said, "You search the Scriptures because you think that in them you have eternal life; and it is they that bear witness about Me" (John 5:39). From Genesis to Revelation, the Bible's story is the story of God saving us by preparing to send His Son, sending Him, raising Him from the dead, and preparing once again to send Him on the Last Day. Knowing this gives us a great leg up in reading the Bible profitably and helps us avoid the common pitfalls of taking the Bible out of its intended context.

But there are two more ways to talk about knowing the biblical story that I think are necessary for profitable Bible reading: knowing the basic doctrine of the Bible and knowing the outline of the Bible's storyline. It's all about Jesus—His story as the coming Lord in the Old Testament and His teaching in the New Testament—but the more detail you know about the story of Jesus, the more you will get out of daily Bible reading.

Core Teachings

In the time of the Reformation, the printing press was in its infancy. Books were still, by and large, something only the privileged classes could enjoy. Even after movable type made books much cheaper, the Bible had to be translated into the native language of the people. And even after that occurred, the result was something like an "information dump." Imagine going from being discouraged to ever read the Bible under the medieval papacy to suddenly having the whole thing dumped into your lap. Where do you begin?

Luther saw the problem as well—and he was the guy who translated the whole Bible for the people in the first place! His solution to the "too much information" complaint was the Small Catechism, which came to be referred to as the Layman's Bible. We would still do well today to read our Bibles with the catechism in the other hand.

The catechism is something like a CliffsNotes edition of the Bible: the key doctrinal concepts, drawn straight from the Scriptures, are all laid out for you. You don't have to worry that you are getting a slanted view of the Scriptures, either, because the catechism itself is nothing but a collection of Bible verses. Luther also added simple explanations (the

"What Does This Mean" questions) to help parents teach the catechism to their children. The catechism itself is simply an executive summary of the Bible in the Bible's own language.

Nor can we outgrow the need to review this basic outline and summary of Christian truth. Luther writes,

> Here am I, an old doctor of theology and a preacher, and certainly as competent in Scripture as such smart alecks. At least I ought to be. Yet even I must become a child; and early each day I recite aloud to myself the Lord's Prayer, the Ten Commandments, the Creed, and whatever lovely psalms and verses I may choose, just as we teach and train children to do. Besides, I must deal with Scripture and fight with the devil every day. I dare not say in my heart: "The Lord's Prayer is worn out; you know the Ten Commandments; you can recite the Creed." I study them daily and remain a pupil of the Catechism. I feel, too, that this helps me a lot, and I am convinced by experience that God's Word can never be entirely mastered.[1]

---

[1] Martin Luther, *Luther's Works. Vol. 14.* Edited by Jaroslav Pelikan (St. Louis: Concordia, 1958), p. 8.

So as you begin your daily commitment to reading a portion of the Scriptures, pull down that dusty catechism from the bookshelf and read a portion of it every day at the start of your Bible reading time. That way your Bible reading will never be disconnected from the basics of the faith, and your Bible reading will flesh out that outline as you continue to read.

And don't neglect to keep that catechism on hand for another purpose: as an excellent glossary of terms. Confused about what the following words might mean: *justification*, *sanctification*, *grace*, *redemption*? You can find them and many others in the back of *Luther's Small Catechism with Explanation* and get not only short definitions, but also detailed discussions with Bible verses to back up the definitions.

Of course, a good study Bible, such as *The Lutheran Study Bible*, can perform this function, too, and also provide maps, timelines, notes, and a concordance.

The Storyline

Back to the idea of not being able to follow a conversation unless you have some kind of idea about the topic at hand—the Bible covers thousands of years of history over the course of sixty-six books. How do you keep all of that straight?

Again, we can look to that great educator Luther for an idea. Beginning in 1522 and extending all the way up to the last year of his life, Luther printed a *Personal Prayer Book* for the Christians of his day.[2] It included a catechism, a sermon on dying, other prayers and psalms, and fifty-two woodcuts that summarized the key stories of the Bible.

The idea is to lay a foundation for further biblical study by first learning the superstructure of the Scriptures through these key stories. Below I'll speak about three ways of reading the Scriptures—short daily devotions, in-depth daily devotions, and cover-to-cover reading—but no matter which you chose for your Jesus-centered life, I recommend that you first review these stories from Luther's list. They will almost all be familiar to you, but in rereading them in order you will begin to impress into your mind the overall shape of the Bible's story from Eden to Judgment Day.

The beauty of Luther's selections lies not only in the framework they pride for understanding the Scriptures, but also in their brevity. I have supplemented his list of Old Testament stories with a review of the history of Israel after Israel enters the Promised Land; these additions are in square brackets.

---

2   Martin Luther, *Luther's Works. Vol. 43*. Edited by Gustav K. Wiencke (St. Louis: Concordia, 1968), pp. 3–45.

OLD TESTAMENT STORIES

1. Creation of the World.   Genesis 1
2. Creation of Man.   Genesis 2
3. Fall of Man.   Genesis 3
4. Cain and Abel.   Genesis 4
5. Noah's Ark.   Genesis 6–9
6. Tower of Babel.   Genesis 11
7. Call of Abraham.   Genesis 12
8. Destruction of Sodom.   Genesis 18–19
9. Sacrifice of Isaac.   Genesis 22
10. Joseph.   Genesis 37–50
11. Call of Moses.   Exodus 1–3
12. Plagues against Egypt.   Exodus 7–11
13. Passover.   Exodus 12
14. The Parting of the Red Sea.   Exodus 14
15. Manna from Heaven.   Exodus 16
16. The Ten Commandments.   Exodus 20
17. The Bronze Serpent.   Numbers 21
[18. The Judges.   Judges 2–3]
[19. Israel Asks for a King.   1 Samuel 8]
[20. David and Goliath.   1 Samuel 16–17]
[21. David and Bathsheba.   2 Samuel 11–12]
[22. King Solomon Asks for Wisdom.   1 Kings 3]
[23. Solomon's Apostasy.   1 Kings 11]
[24. The Divided Kingdom.   1 Kings 12]
[25. The Northern Kingdom Is
    Destroyed.   2 Kings 17]

NEW TESTAMENT STORIES

19. Jesus before Pontius Pilate.	John 18:28–40
20. Passion and Crucifixion.	John 19
21. Resurrection.	John 20:1–18
22. Jesus Shows Himself to Thomas.	John 20:19–31
23. Ascension.	Luke 24; Acts 1
24. Pentecost.	Acts 2
25. Judgment Day and Resurrection.	Matthew 25; 1 Corinthians 15; 1 Thessalonians 4:13–18

If you are going to take the concrete step of striking out on a new regimen of daily Bible reading, then I strongly suggest that you start here. It really is vital that you get the full scope and arc of the biblical story in your head before you try to read through the whole of the Sacred Scriptures from cover to cover. Reading these stories in order may take you quite a while at ten to fifteen minutes a day, but it will be very worthwhile. If you feel like you already have a pretty good grasp of this basic biblical narrative, then just skimming through the stories that don't sound familiar to you will probably get the job done.

Timeline

In addition to this list of biblical narratives, I also find that my parishioners benefit from committing just a few key dates to memory. Once again, this helps you to keep the story straight no matter what section of the Bible you are reading. Most of the dates here are approximate—for example, the exodus actually occurred in 1452 BC, but I list it here at 1500 BC for the sake of easy memorization. This is just an outline, trail markers along the way of history so that you can keep the whole biblical story straight.

Creation, Fall, and Flood—some thousands of years BC; traditionally the creation is set at:	4004 BC
Abraham:	2000 BC
Moses and the Exodus:	1500 BC
Time of the Judges:	1500–1000 BC
King David:	1000 BC
The Kings of Judah and Israel:	1000–721 BC
Northern Kingdom (Israel) Destroyed:	721 BC
Jerusalem Destroyed, Judah Exiled:	586 BC
Temple Rebuilt:	516 BC
The Last Prophet (Malachi):	400 BC
Judah subjugated under the Persians, Greeks, and Maccabees:	400–63 BC
Judah under Roman rule:	63 BC–AD 637
Birth of Christ:	4 BC
Crucifixion and Resurrection:	AD 33
Deaths of Peter and Paul:	AD 68
Romans destroy Jerusalem:	AD 70
Book of Revelation:	AD 100

Translations and Study Bibles

At this point it should be clear what an advantage a study Bible can be to the Christian who wants to make a serious effort at abiding in Jesus' Word for the sake of a Jesus-centered life. A solid study Bible contains historical introductions to each book, outlines of each book, a complete historical outline, cross references from one passage to another, a glossary of terms, a concordance, and more.

But each study Bible includes something else: a perspective. There are some study Bibles, for example, that were compiled by people who don't believe in the Bible as the Word of God. In such works you will find notes advocating evolution, explaining away difficult passages, and generally trying to erode any true faith in God. You don't want one of those. Nor do you want a study Bible that is going to approach the Scriptures from the position of faulty Christian theology.

That's why I was so excited when *The Lutheran Study Bible* came out a few years ago. This was a study Bible with all the bells and whistles that I could recommend to my parishioners without reservation. It is certainly an investment worth making if you are planning to jump into serious biblical study. No study Bible can replace the need for a live, interactive study of the Scriptures with your pastor—in fact, I find that it's just those parishioners who have invested in *The Lutheran Study Bible* that come to class with even more and better questions! A quality study Bible leads you more deeply into the Scriptures and, therefore, gives you even more to think about. And the more biblical doctrine and narrative you understand, the more you will want to understand and seek out your pastor's Bible class to find the answers.

If you pick up *The Lutheran Study Bible*, that will take care of another decision about Bible reading: which translation of the Scriptures should you choose? There are many fine translations on the market, but there are also many translations that are really nothing more than paraphrases, and, worst of all, there are translations with theological axes to grind that simply can't be trusted.

So what is a quality Bible translation? When I am really stuck on a hard bit of Greek or Hebrew and I turn to several English translations to help me determine what the original text means, I find that the good old King James Version is more accurate than the other translations nine times out of ten. Yet, that doesn't really help the average modern Christian for whom the KJV is flat out puzzling. That's why I usually recommend the very translation that serves as the basis of *The Lutheran Study Bible*, the English Standard Version. This is a solid translation undertaken by a group of traditional Christians specifically with the idea of being in the tradition and lineage of the venerable King James Version. Even if you don't pick up *The Lutheran Study Bible* (but you should!), I would still recommend buying an English Standard Version translation of the Bible.

Visit cph.org/tlsb to learn more about *The Lutheran Study Bible.*

Three Methods of Daily Scripture Reading

You've set aside the time for daily Scripture reading, you've reviewed the basic biblical narratives, you've got a few key dates in your head, and you've even picked up a study Bible. Now what? Do you just start with Genesis 1:1 and plow through the Scriptures?

READING IT THROUGH

That's certainly one way of doing it—making the decision to read through all of Scripture in a given span of time (two years seems to work well for many people). There is much that is laudable about this method of daily Scripture reading, but there are also drawbacks.

The chief difficulty with the plan of reading through the Bible over a certain number of weeks, months, or years is that it is so easy to get discouraged and bogged down. Some books, such as the Gospels, Judges, and Genesis, seem to skip right along and are a joy to read. This is because those books are chiefly a collection of stories, and stories keep us interested with their plots and characters. But then when you come to books of poetry like Isaiah or Job, books of minute ceremonial detail like Leviticus, or books of cryptic prophecy like Ezekiel or Revelation, you may find that your Bible reading time has become a real chore.

If you decide that reading through the Bible cover to cover is for you, then here is what you can do to escape these common pitfalls.

First, don't start with the cover-to-cover plan right way, instead start with the list of Bible narratives I listed above. This will ease you into the habit of daily Bible reading with the easier-to-read narratives. By the time you finish that list, you will find that the more difficult sections of the Scripture will be manageable precisely because you know that not all of the Bible is so difficult! "If I just hang on through Leviticus, I know some good stories are right around the corner in Judges." In fact, once you begin reading the "difficult" portions, you'll see how they hook up with the familiar stories you already know and they won't be so "difficult" anymore!

Second, you will have to be doubly disciplined. Since you will be reading long portions of poetry, prophecy, and history that may not grab your attention as fully as a story of Jesus healing a blind man, you will need to be all the more serious about making time for daily Bible reading and sticking to it.

Finally, if you skip a day, don't try to catch up just to make your "deadline." Setting a goal of a year, two years, or three years to read through the Bible is great, but it's not the end of the world if you have to tack on a month or even a year to your goal. You are much more likely to miss your goal if you regularly try to do two or three days' worth of reading in one day. If you miss a day, you miss a day—just pick up where you left off.

The rewards of a cover-to-cover reading of the Bible are real. A parishioner of mine finished his reading of the Scriptures a couple of months ago, and it was exciting to listen to his updates each week during the process when we spoke after church. What I noticed most was how he was beginning to see the connections in all the small and out of the way places of the Bible. And the questions he had! You see, when you read through cover to cover, you are not skipping any of the places that make you scratch your head. What's up with Hebrews 6? And how on earth do we understand Jephthah's daughter? He had great questions for me precisely because he was struggling with the whole biblical text.

BITE-SIZED READING

If feasting on the whole Word of God in a given amount of time sounds like too much for you right now, then you can go to the other end of the spectrum and try the bite-sized approach. This is probably the most popular method of daily Bible reading with my parishioners and is the sort of daily reading encouraged by devotionals like *Portals of Prayer*.

The idea here is to focus on a given Bible theme chosen by the author of the devotional and to read short portions of the Scriptures that support this theme. The devotional writer chooses

Portals of Prayer is a quarterly magazine of daily devotions available in print and online editions from CPH.

the passage(s) to read and includes a brief explanation of the text. There are also usually prayers to go along with each lesson and devotion. (We'll deal with praying through the Scriptures in the next chapter.)

I think this is popular among my parishioners because it is so manageable and accessible. It's manageable because the readings tend to be short—just a paragraph or two. Instead of the ten- to fifteen-minute minimum required to study a chapter or two of the Scriptures, my parishioners know that they can pick up *Portals of Prayer* and cruise through the reading in just a minute or two.

Such a method is also immediately accessible because the devotion serves as a brief explanation of the text. If you are reading through the Bible cover to cover, there is no accompanying devotional to guide you through the reading and pull a lesson from it for you. Instead, you have to do that on your own or with the help of the notes of a study Bible, which for any given passage of the Bible will be much longer than the brief devotion in *Portals of Prayer*.

The main downside to the devotional approach is the other side of the brevity coin: you aren't getting that much of the Bible text each day. True, each day you are getting a solid Law and Gospel biblical thought put in your head and heart, but you are not digging much deeper than that either. The simple fact is that there is only so much you can learn at the rate of ten to twenty verses per day.

The second downside to the bite-sized approach is that you are at the mercy of the devotional writer. You are going to be reading exactly those passages that this author chose and nothing else. This makes choosing the devotional a very important decision. But even beyond the fact that the author is choosing the biblical passages, you will also be at his or her mercy when it comes to the devotional thoughts that are added to the Scripture passages for the day. How trustworthy is this author? Is he or she asking the right questions? Does he or she know what the passage truly means?

If you have never had the habit of daily Bible reading before, then I think you would be well served to start with the bite-sized approach after you read through Luther's list of biblical narratives to prime your pump. Eventually, as you become accustomed to the daily rhythm of reading the Scriptures, you may want more. When that happens, you can easily add to your daily routine.

A MIDDLE WAY

If you are reading this book, I won't be surprised if you are already going to Bible class and reading at least a brief passage of Scripture every day. Maybe you've even read the Scriptures all the way through before. If that is the case, and you are looking for something different to further enrich your Jesus-centered life, then I suggest you strike out on the time-honored path of the breviary.

The what? A breviary is a traditional method of staying connected to the Word of God throughout the year that splits the difference between a bare read-through-the-Bible approach and a quick-daily-devotion approach. A breviary contains good-sized but manageable readings from the Bible for each day, as well as devotions from classic Christian sources.

In other words, you will be reading through the greater portion of Scripture each year, but not the whole Scripture. You will be reading a devotion every day, though not a devotion from a contemporary living author, but rather a meatier devotion from the greatest saints, preachers, and evangelists of Christian history.

There is only one breviary that I recommend: *Treasury of Daily Prayer*. I can't say enough about the blessings of this collection of prayers, readings, devotions, the catechism, and the entire Psalter. I know the pious thing to say when you are asked what book you would want on a desert island is the Bible, but I would be sorely tempted to say the *Treasury*. It's got nearly the whole Bible in it, plus all these other wonderful resources. In any given week, I might read devotions from Martin Luther, St. Ignatius, Herman Sasse, and Bernard of Clairvaux, all while reading through the whole New Testament in a year and a great portion of the Old Testament, including all the Major Prophets and history.

The *Treasury* has something to offer you no matter what your background in daily Bible reading—greater depth for those who have used shorter devotionals in the past, greater focus and direction for those who have read through the Bible cover to cover. And for those who may be starting out in daily devotions, what you have in the *Treasury* is truly scalable. If two chapters (one Old Testament and one New Testament), a psalm, a devotion, a hymn,

Visit cph.org/prayer to learn more about the *Treasury of Daily Prayer*.

and a prayer a day seems like too much for you, then the first year just read either the Old Testament or the New Testament lesson along with the devotion. Or just read the psalm and the devotion. Or just read the New Testament lesson and the hymn. This book is infinitely adjustable to the time and effort you want to devote to your new daily Bible reading time.

The Only Bible You Get to Keep

"For God so loved the world . . ." (John 3:16)

"If we say we have no sin . . ." (1 John 1:8)

"All our righteous deeds are like . . ." (Isaiah 64:6)

"For by grace you have been saved . . ." (Ephesians 2:8)

Can you complete any of those dot-dot-dots? How many other Bible passages can you pull out of your memory? The fact of the matter is that until you can pull some of the Bible from your memory, you don't own a Bible at all, at least not a Bible you can keep and use for life. If you live to a ripe old age, your eyesight will weaken, or your mind may get a little fuzzy, or your hands may get too arthritic to hold up a book or even a sheet of paper. If you are dependent on a printed Bible for the Word of God, you may then find yourself shut out of its comfort and peace. Likewise, a Christian should always be ready to meet a time of danger, illness, injury, or the need of another with the Word of God. By the very nature of such emergencies, there is no time to dig out a Bible and flip to the page you want, even if you happen to have one in your pocket or on your phone. The Word of God in that situation will either be engraved on your memory or not there at all.

Due to the church service, you already have a great deal more of the Bible memorized than you might think. If you are making the time to center your life in Jesus by being in His house each week, then you are already having the Word of God burned into your memory. "Holy, holy, holy Lord God of Sabaoth" (*LSB*, p. 195)—that's Isaiah 6:3. "If we say we have no sin . . ." (*LSB*, p. 151)—that's from 1 John 1:8. "O Christ, Thou Lamb of God . . ." (*LSB*, p. 198)—that's John 1:29. So a good place to start with your intentional memorization of the Bible is with the hymnal. Borrow one from church if you don't have one at home, and open up to the Divine Service. There in the margins you'll see the citation for the Bible passages you've been memorizing your whole life!

The best way to add to your internal Bible is to key your memorization to weekly worship. By memorizing one verse from each Sunday's Divine Service in the week following, you will connect your daily life of Bible reading to the Church's heart and soul: the worship of the triune God.

Each Sunday in church, we read through specific readings from the lectionary. The lectionary orders the Church Year. Each December 25 is Christmas, which is preceded by the Sundays of Advent, and each of those days has an Old Testament, New Testament, and Gospel lesson, along with some psalm verses in the

A lectionary is a collection of appointed Scriptures for use in the Divine Service.

Introit, Psalm, Gradual, and Verse. If you want to look at all of these laid out for the course of the year, you just need to pick up a copy of the hymnal and have a look (*LSB*, pp. xiv–xxiii). Ask your pastor if you are on the one-year or the three-year lectionary in your church.

But there is no need to look up the whole listing of a year's lectionary to do the weekly memorization of verses. Just select one of the verses that was read during the Divine Service for that week's memory work. I recommend choosing a verse from the Gospel lesson, as the Gospel is always the focal point of the Divine Service. Pick the verse that seems the most memorable or central or that just catches your attention. You will be amazed at how that verse will stick with you year to year as this Sunday in the lectionary comes up again and again. You are not only putting great verses in your internal Bible, you are also learning the rhythm of the story the Church is telling through its cycle of feasts and festivals.

Here are some easy steps to help engrave the Word of God on your heart.

First, write down the verse to be memorized that week. I recommend investing in a set of index cards for this purpose. Since you are keying your memory verses to the worship service, you'll want to save them from year to year.

Second, use this index card each week as your bookmark in your Bible, prayer book, or devotional book.

Third, each day when you sit down to do your Bible reading, you'll have your memory verse right there as the bookmark. Simply read the verse aloud before you start your daily reading and again when you put the bookmark back at the end of your reading.

Writing the verse out at the beginning of the week and saying it aloud twice each day for the rest of the week uses multiple pathways in your brain to engrave that Word of God more firmly in your memory. If you do just this much, you will be amazed at how well these verses will stick with you—and how they will come back to you in times of need or distress in your life and in the life of your friends and family.

So that's it—no quizzes, not a lot of time required, just brief daily repetition of verses from Sunday, and you will soon have an internal Bible that no one can take away from you and that you can always have immediately in any time of need.

Beyond the Basics: The Apocrypha

If you read through the whole Old Testament from Genesis to Malachi, you will read a lot about the temple, the sacrifices, the kings of Israel, and the promise of the coming Christ. But you will not read anything about Pharisees, Sadducees, or Roman centurions—things that form the backbone of many stories in the New Testament. Where did all this stuff come from?

Remember our timeline from earlier? Look at that big gap between Malachi and the birth of Christ: there are about four hundred years between the Testaments! What would you be missing about American history if you skipped everything between Jamestown and September 11, 2001? Well, a lot of history about Pharisees, Romans, and so forth happened in that four-century span between the last chapter of Malachi and the first chapter of Matthew.

If you want to fill in the gaps of your understanding about this intertestamental time period, then you will need to supplement your Bible reading with a look at the Apocrypha. This collection of books written by various Israelites in those four hundred years between the testaments is not on the same level with the Word of God, but throughout the years it has been included between the covers of Christian Bibles as supplemental reading. That's right where Luther put it in his translation of the Scriptures and where every German Luther Bible ever used in the Lutheran Church had it as well.

Why it fell out of our English Bibles is a long story, and that story goes beyond our purposes here, but the good news is that the Apocrypha can once again be profitably read by English-speaking Lutherans in a new edition, *The Apocrypha: The Lutheran Edition with Notes*. I recommended this book to my regular Sunday Bible class folks who are already enjoying an active daily Scripture reading habit. This is, after all, supplemental reading. First, make the time for and get into the habit of daily Bible reading. Once you have that firmly established, you will no doubt enjoy reading through the Apocrypha—especially the historical books (1 and 2 Maccabees) that explain the history of Israel between the Testaments.

Foundation

The Nicene Creed sums it up best: "I believe in the Holy Spirit . . . who spoke by the prophets." The Holy Spirit does not speak to us while we sit on the couch watching football, are out on the golf course, or down at the mall shopping. We should not look for the Holy Spirit to drop messages to us from the sky or in our dreams. God has promised to speak to us through the prophets—that is, through the Scriptures. This is our foundation of truth. If we abide in the Word of Jesus, we are truly His disciples. So make the time and set out to gain the blessings that God has stored up for you in His Word today.

Key Points

- God promises to bless you through His Word.

- The Word of God is a Means of Grace.

- Knowing the outline of the overall story of the Bible is necessary to get a lot out of daily reading.

- Knowing the basic doctrine of the Bible (Small Catechism) is also necessary to get a lot out of daily reading.

Discussion Questions

1. Have you tried to read through the Bible before? Did you make it?

2. What is your favorite Bible story?

3. Do you like reading the Old Testament or the New Testament better? Why?

4. What book of the Bible are you most excited about studying?

Action Steps

1. Attend your pastor's weekly Bible class.

2. Set aside ten to fifteen minutes a day for Scripture reading. Make a plan for what sort of reading you want to embark on, whether it's read-through-the-Bible, *a devotional book or periodical*, or a *prayer book*.

3. Get a good study Bible.

4. Keep the bulletin from the weekly church service so you can make memory verse cards from the Gospel lesson.

5. Review the Small Catechism.

Take a Breath: Where Prayer Comes From

> Now Jesus was praying in a certain place, and
> when He finished, one of His disciples said to Him,
> "Lord, teach us to pray, as John taught His disciples."
> And He said to them, "When you pray, say:
> 'Father, hallowed be Your name. . . .'" (Luke 11:1–2)

If Baptism is our birth into the kingdom of God, if the Word of God is our true spiritual milk, if the holy body and blood of our Lord's Supper is a Christian's real food and drink, then prayer is our breath. And if it is breath, then it is given to us, for in God's Word no one may take a breath unless they have first received it as a gift.

That's what happened in the Garden of Eden. Adam received God's own breath in order that he might breathe and be a living soul. God breathed in, Adam breathed out.

In the Book of Ezekiel, when the prophet saw the vision of the dry bones of Israel, God instructed him to call on the breath that it might enter those lifeless bodies and revive them. God breathed in; Israel breathed out.

In the first chapter, we saw how we receive God's breath, His Word, as we hear what He has said to us and as we say it back to Him in the Divine Service. God breathes in; the liturgy breathes out. And if God does not breathe in, we can neither inhale nor exhale. Like a man with a boulder on his chest, we do not have the power to draw in our own air; like a disoriented ocean diver who cannot read the labels on his diving tanks, we don't know what we should breathe.

So it is and must be with our prayers, as the Gospel quotation at the beginning of the chapter teaches. In a rare moment of clarity, the disciples get something right: "Lord, teach us to pray." Why teach us? Isn't prayer just asking for what you want? Who needs to be taught that? Ah, but like Adam in the garden and Ezekiel's army of dry bones, we are empty, having been hollowed out by our sin, our brokenness, and our rebellion. We have nothing to say to our Father in heaven; His Son must first fill us up. And what had Jesus been doing right before His disciples asked Him how they should pray? He was Himself praying! You see, our prayer life must come from our Lord's prayer life, because left on our own we are hollow people—well, not exactly hollow, we are quite full of ourselves, but quite empty when it comes to the things of God.

So how does Jesus breathe into us and fill us up when it comes to prayer? How does Jesus respond to His disciples' request about teaching them to pray? He does not give a lecture on the metaphysics of communicating with God. Nor does he encourage us to just bare our hearts to God and say whatever comes to mind; He knows our hearts too well to tell us that! He knows that we will ask for little, mean, and spiteful things: for the death of enemies instead of for their repentance, for the growth of our purses instead of our hearts, for the fulfillment of our every petty desire and lust instead of for the coming of His kingdom and the doing of His will. Jesus, like every good writer and storyteller, shows us how to pray instead of just telling us. "Our Father, who art in heaven, hallowed be Thy name, Thy kingdom come, Thy will be done on earth as it is in heaven . . ." (see Matthew 11 and Luke 6). Now filled with His Word, His breath, His prayer, we may breathe back to Him the same words, His words, our Lord's words. For this is not my prayer, it is not your prayer, it is the Lord's Prayer.

The Promise of Prayer

It's here that our reflection on prayer should start: Jesus breathes in; we breathe out. Like a parent with a toddler learning to talk, Jesus speaks and we repeat. But this isn't glamorous. Isn't there some trick? Shouldn't *my* prayer come from *my* heart? How can I pray these words that are not mine? Why can't I name and claim what I want? Praise be to God that He does not invite us to "name it and claim it." Praise be to Him for His promise in 1 John 5:14: "And this is the confidence that we have toward Him, that if we ask anything according to His will He hears us." Praise be to our Lord that He tells us to pray, "Thy will be done," and that in the Garden of Gethsemane He Himself prayed, "Father, . . . not as I will, but as You will" (Matthew 26:39).

But what kind of promise is this? We are tempted to say, "It's a bum deal if ever I've heard one." Like Henry Ford who boasted that his customers could have a Model T in any color they wanted so long as it was black, God says we can have whatever we want so long as it is in accord with what He wants. When God does not answer our prayers in the way we want at the bedside of a child dying of leukemia, in the prison of Grandma's chronic arthritis, or in the countless other miseries of this fallen world, this seems cold comfort. If these situations are what God wants, then I most certainly do not want it! I do not want the dying and the killing and the crying and the hurting and the rejection and the sickness and the pain. If this is God's will, then I want to pray against it, raise my fist against Him. How can this be God's will? How can He expect me to ask for it?

But if we ask these questions, we have forgotten who gave us this prayer. This is not some spiritual guru on TV who will pass to dust like everyone else. This is Jesus the Christ, God in the flesh come down to rid us of the misery we have caused in His perfect creation. Are you angry at what seems to be the will of God? Has this made it hard for you to pray? Then remember the Garden of Gethsemane and the Father's true will—a will so strong and so paradoxically merciful and just that it sent His innocent, holy Son to die on the cross to take upon Himself all the dying, killing, crying, hurting, rejection, sickness, and pain.

Do you want to know God's will? Do you want to know what you are praying for when you ask for it? Do you want to know why asking for anything contrary to it is unimaginably horrid? Then look to the cross on which the Prince of glory died. His will was His own death on your behalf. And while we are in this vale of tears, we will still suffer the effects of our rebellious broken existence. But His glorious resurrection and His ascension into heaven to prepare a place for us there is His firm promise that one day He will wipe away every tear from our eyes.

So pray. Pray for His good and gracious will. Pray as dear children ask their dear Father. For His will is to break and hinder every evil plan and pur-

When I survey the wondrous cross
On which the Prince of Glory died,
My richest gain I count but loss
And pour contempt on all my pride.
(*LSB* 425:1)

pose of the devil, the world, and our frail, sinful flesh. His will is to strengthen and keep us firm in His Word and faith until we die. Do not be afraid that you are unworthy to approach your Father in heaven. He Himself has invited you to pray. He Himself has sent His Son to redeem you, "not with gold or silver, but with His holy, precious blood and with His innocent suffering and death" (Small Catechism, Second Article). Thus, we can approach His throne of grace with confidence.

Pray. For He is the true Father from whom all fatherhood on earth draws its name. Even our earthly fathers, those poor and wicked reflections of the true Father, know how to give good gifts to their children. If a son asks for an egg, he will not receive a stone. If a daughter asks for a fish, her father will not give her a serpent. (See Luke 11:11–13.) So do not allow schedules and meetings and meals and traffic and homework and practice and TV and everything else to push prayer out of your life. Prayer is the breath of your Jesus-centered life. Your heavenly Father yearns to give you good things, so approach His throne of grace with confidence.

You see, God is the best friend we have. He is the true Friend. And even our friends, those petty reflections of God's neighborly love, are accustomed to giving us what we ask for when we are in a fix, even if it is just because they would be ashamed to appear ungenerous. But your Father in heaven is generosity itself, not sparing His own Son to save your sinful, broken soul. So don't be discouraged if you think God has let you down before. The fact that His ways are not our ways is not an empty, pious statement but the purest Good News. For if He undertook our will as His own, sin and pain and disaster would not recede but blossom. No, we must trust His love and if ever we doubt it—which is Satan's most earnest desire—we must fix our eyes on our crucified Lord and view His love mingled with sorrow flowing down. We must approach the throne of grace with confidence.

Breathe in God's good will and good Word. Ask, because every good will be given you in this life and the next. Seek, and you will find God's good and gracious will. Knock, and the door to the kingdom of the Father will be opened. Do not be afraid that your words will be in vain, for they are not your words! You are praying the words of Christ in the power of the Spirit's new birth of Baptism. As you breathe in the Word of God and breathe it out, your Jesus-centered life will grow.

Make Time

All that is why you should make the time for real daily prayer, and not only "Come, Lord Jesus" before meals and "Now I lay me down to sleep" before bed. Below I'll talk very specifically about how that works on a daily basis, but before you are motivated to set aside time for Word-centered, mature prayer, you must know all this about God's Word as your breath, about Jesus' love for you, and about His promises to hear your voice. It's just like what we said about being in God's Word daily and making the time to be in worship each week: there are great blessings and promises from God attached to prayer.

How much time? Just as for daily Bible reading, I advise you to start with a manageable goal in the ten-to-fifteen-minute range. That's ten to fifteen minutes of uninterrupted time where you can be alone and dedicate the time to prayer.

If that doesn't sound like much, you may find that it's actually a tall order once you try to set it aside. I'm blessed in that part of my job is to pray. It's easy for me to set aside the time to pray on any day that I have a church service to prepare for or work to do around the school or office. But there is no doubt about which day of the week I struggle most to set aside the time to pray: Saturday. That's usually my day off. I'm not at church and I'm not in my office very often on Saturdays. So I had to come up with a plan to set aside time for prayer on that day—it's when my older kids, who can be left alone in the tub, take their Saturday bath. At that time I can go into my room and pray without interruption (but I can still hear them splashing around in there if there should be an emergency!).

Speaking of kids, my wife, as a stay-at-home mom, also has to be very deliberate about setting aside time for prayer, because kids *never* want to let a mother have a moment's peace! If you work a nine-to-five job, it will be the same for you; you will need to be deliberate to set some time aside. In fact, everyone's schedule is busy: work, entertainment, getting kids here and there, meal preparation, jobs to do around the house—it never ends!

Setting aside the time for prayer is perhaps even more difficult than setting aside the time for daily Bible reading. I can do my daily devotional reading in the living room while the kids flit in and out and my wife asks me if I have an idea for supper. It's nice when I can do my reading in my office and really focus, but it's not absolutely necessary every day. If I've had the kind of day where I just can't get that time by myself to read, reading my *Treasury* on the couch, on the bleachers, or while I wait in the parking lot to pick somebody up usually works fine.

With prayer, though, you really do need to set aside a time you can be alone. For many people the simplest, if not the easiest, way to do this may be to set your alarm ten minutes earlier than usual and use that time for prayer. But wherever you find the time for prayer, make it a daily priority and stick with it.

Daily Rhythm

In the Small Catechism, Luther recommends a daily rhythm to our prayer life. He tells us to pray in the morning when we get up, at meals, and in the evening before we go to bed. He also gives a brief outline of what each of those prayer times look like. In the morning and evening, he advises you to make the sign of the cross (more on that later) and pray the Apostles' Creed and the Lord's Prayer. At mealtime he suggests a given Bible verse, the Lord's Prayer, and a meal prayer.

These are good disciplines to get into a daily rhythm of prayer and yet another reason that you should pull that old catechism off the shelf. Yet Luther's outline of daily prayer in the catechism should not be taken as the be-all and end-all of a Christian's daily prayers. You should also set aside that ten to fifteen minutes for further prayers—not just any prayers but prayers that breathe in the Word of God and then breathe it back to the heavenly Father who gave His Word. What follow here are several ways to get at that biblical, mature manner of prayer.

Ways to Pray

A WHOLE-BODY EXERCISE

As I just mentioned, Luther's Small Catechism advises you to make use of your whole body in prayer. The Daily Prayers section suggests standing or kneeling, making the sign of the cross, and then saying aloud, "In the name of the Father and of the Son and of the Holy Spirit. Amen." These are physical actions that involve your whole person—body and soul—in your prayers. Of course you can pray silently while driving in the car, sitting at your desk, or lying in your bed—and Paul encourages us to "pray without ceasing" (1 Thessalonians 5:17), so any time is a good time to pray. The overwhelming number of examples in the Bible of praying include a bodily posture (kneeling and standing) and speaking aloud. First and foremost, there is the example of Jesus who knelt, with His face down, and prayed aloud in Gethsemane, but just about every other example of prayer in the Bible likewise includes speaking aloud and a posture of humility toward ourselves and honor toward God.

Why might that be? Because we are not just minds; we are persons, each consisting of a body and a soul. In our Sunday worship, we worship with our bodies—standing, kneeling, singing, speaking—and our prayer life should be no different. Try it out during the ten to fifteen minutes you have set aside for private prayer. Praying out loud like this also fits better with the model of prayer that we'll discuss next based on praying through the Word of God.

PRAYING THROUGH THE LORD'S PRAYER

The Lord's Prayer is not only a prayer to be prayed devoutly but a framework for all devout prayer. The Lord's Prayer teaches us to order our prayers according to God's priorities and to pray for what we need in a way that God wishes to hear. Therefore, one of the best disciplines for praying is to pray the Lord's Prayer one petition at a time and then let your private prayers flow from that petition. The greatest aid in learning to do this is the Small Catechism.

You pray this way in three steps.

1. Kneel or stand with your catechism in front of you, and first pray one line of the Lord's Prayer: "Our Father who art in heaven."

2. Read the explanation of the line in the Small Catechism: "With these words God tenderly invites us to believe that He is our true Father and that we are His true children, so that with all boldness and confidence we may ask Him as dear children ask their dear father" (Lord's Prayer, Introduction).

3. Now let your own personal prayer flow from this part of the Lord's Prayer based on the catechism's explanation. For example, at this point you could pray a thanksgiving for God calling you His true child and being your true Father. Or it might be a confession of not having the "boldness and confidence" that you ought to have in praying toward God.

4. Go on to the next line of the Lord's Prayer, following the same steps.

Each time you follow this exercise of praying through the Lord's Prayer, your prayer at any given line will probably be different. That's the point of all these exercises in breathing in and breathing out prayer: the Word of God you are praying will change you and interact with you at different points in your life.

PRAYING THE PSALMS

Right alongside the Lord's Prayer in importance for deepening your prayer life stand the Psalms. These are the God-given prayer book. In the Psalms you will find all the range of human emotion and suffering. You will find a voice for whatever is troubling you, whatever is causing you joy, whatever is bringing you grief or making anger well up in your heart. It's all there.

The procedure for praying through a psalm is just the same as I mentioned above for praying through the Lord's Prayer. Pray a verse, and then let that verse guide you to pray about something in your life—whether it moves you to pray a confession, a thanksgiving, or a request. Very likely each psalm you pray will lead you to pray in all these ways.

I don't pray through the Lord's Prayer and a psalm in this verse-by-verse manner everyday—though that would certainly be a good discipline. On many days I simply pray the Lord's Prayer and a psalm without adding my own personal confessions, thanksgivings, and petitions after each verse. But I do find that praying in this way has changed the shape of my normal daily prayers even when I don't begin those normal daily prayers with this verse-by-verse exercise. I find that the order of the Lord's Prayer and the Psalms has soaked into the rest of my prayer life. It's hard to think about praying in any other way than first starting with praise for God and a confession of my need for forgiveness and then asking for spiritual and earthly blessings.

I would encourage you to include a psalm—whether prayed just as it is written or in this verse-by-verse manner—every day in your ten to fifteen minutes of private prayer. Just begin at Psalm 1 and start praying. When you get to the longer psalms, break them up over several days. Or use the *Treasury of Daily Prayer*, which includes a collection of psalm verses at the beginning of each day's devotion. I most enjoy reading straight through the Psalms. You will be amazed at how the psalm on any given day will apply directly to you and give voice to what you wanted to pray about. On many days, the psalm of the day will remind you what you should be praying for, and yet on others, you will find something you had never thought to prayer for and are now so glad you found.

PRAYING THE CATECHISM AND SCRIPTURE

The Lord's Prayer and the Psalms are the natural place to begin talking about prayer and learning to pray by breathing in God's Word and breathing it back to Him. After all, these are the portions of God's Word that are actual prayers. But the same procedure can be used to allow any portion of God's Word to guide your prayers. You simply read the verse, and then let your prayer flow from what the Word of God says.

A good place to start here is with the rest of the cat-echism. For example, you could pick up your catechism and turn to the Fourth Commandment and its meaning: "Honor your father and your mother. *What does this mean?* We should fear and love God so that we do not despise or anger our parents and other authorities, but honor them, serve and obey them, love and cherish them." There is plenty to pray about there: giving thanks for the parents God has given you, con-fessing your own sins of disobedience and disrespect, and asking God to bless your parents and help you to honor them.

The same procedure can be followed for any portion of the catechism. Praying through the catechism about once a year in small installments is a great exercise in allowing the Word of God to shape your prayers. You can follow the same steps with any portion of Scripture that you are reading in your daily devotions.

PRAYING WITH THE CHURCH: HYMNALS AND PRAYER BOOKS

Finally, a survey of ways to pray would not be complete without a look at connecting your individual prayer life with the prayer life of the Church. In Luther's day, and well before that, it was normal for Christians to gather in the church each day in the morning for Matins and in the evening for Vespers. Sadly, this tradition has fallen out of fashion in our day of hyper-busy schedules and commuting long distances to work and church. But you can still connect your life of prayer to the Church's life of prayer with a few tools.

First of all: if you congregation uses them, hang on to the bulletin from Sunday. Often these will include the Collect for Sunday, and I encourage you to make that part of your daily prayers. The Collect is, as the name implies, the collection of the prayers of the people as they relate to the theme of that Sunday. If you are going to take my advice about memorizing key verses from the Gospel lessons of each Sunday, then praying the Collect that matches that Gospel each day only makes sense.

You will find that these prayers follow a certain form: the Collects praise God for some specific goodness or blessing that God has already given and then ask for more blessings today based on that past blessing. For example: "Almighty God, You bless the earth to make it fruitful, bringing forth in abundance whatever is needed for the support of our lives. Prosper the work of farmers and all those who labor to bring food to our table . . ." (Collect for Agriculture, *LSB*, p. 314). If you begin praying these Collects week in and week out, you will find that it becomes a very natural way to pray: you start with God's blessings and your thankfulness for them before asking for new blessings.

More Collects, daily orders of prayer, and specific prayers for specific needs can be found in the hymnal and the *Treasury of Daily Prayer*. I encourage you to include some of these prayers in your ten to fifteen minutes of personal, private

A beautifully done revised and updated Concordia Edition of *Starck's Prayer Book* is available from CPH.

prayer each day. You might also look into classic Lutheran prayer books, such as *Starck's Prayer Book*. It's always a good idea to lean on and learn from the rich history of prayer in the Church. None of us is an island—we are connected since each of us is a member of the Body of Christ. We can always deepen our own understanding of prayer by connecting with the larger Church and learning from Christians of old.

Key Points

- Prayer is the breath of a Christian.

- God promises to answer your prayers in accordance with His will.

- The Lord's Prayer is the perfect outline for daily prayer, and the Psalms are the prayer book of the Bible.

- The prayers of the Church will deepen your prayer life.

Discussion Questions

1. Do you have a story of answered prayer in your life?

2. How about a time when you really prayed hard for something and didn't get it? How do you look back on that now?

3. Whom do you always mention in your daily prayers?

4. Where do you prefer to say your daily prayers?

Action Steps

Set aside ten to fifteen minutes for private prayer
   each day.

2. Keep the bulletin from Sunday so you can pray
   the Collect of the Day all week long.

3. Once a week, use the Lord's Prayer, one petition
   at a time, as the outline for all your daily prayers.
   Once a week, pray through a psalm one verse at a time.
   Once a week, pray through a small section of the catechism.

The first three chapters of this book have been about filling up with Jesus for the Jesus-centered life. You go to the Divine Service to receive the Word of Jesus in the living voice of the Gospel and to be renewed by His Sacraments. You read His Word on your own each day to keep that Word fresh in your heart and continually growing in your mind. You pray God's Word back to Him to call upon His promises and seek His peace.

The last two chapters will be about living out the Jesus-centered life. These chapters are pretty short because the bulk of the work for you to do is in those three main actions of a Christian life. If you follow through with going to church, reading the Word, and praying, then living out your vocation (more on that word below) at work and at home will come naturally. The first three chapters are largely personal; these last two are more public and interpersonal. For each of those tasks—Go to Church, Go Read, Go Pray—I have encouraged you to make time. Now I'm going to talk about the rest of the time—the time out of which you are carving time for church, Word, and prayer. That time belongs to your Jesus-centered life as well.

Not of the World, but Definitely in It

Martin Luther started out his career as a monk. Along with most folks in the Middle Ages, he thought that the best thing you could do with your life was dedicate it to godly service. So Luther locked himself in a monastery to pray and read the Word of God. That was the ideal of a godly life: to separate yourself from the rest of the world. However, Luther came to view the monastery as a most unchristian place. The monks and nuns were actually running away from the godly service that God had designed for His people in the world.

Part of Luther's rediscovery of the Gospel was a rediscovery of joy about life in the world. Christians are filled with Jesus and live salt and light lives in the world He came to save. The fancy word for this is *vocation*, which is Latin for calling. We serve God best in the calling that God has given each of us in the world: that's our vocation.

But I Don't Have a Vocation!

At this point if you are retired or disabled or a stay-at-home mom, you may be thinking, "But I don't have a vocation. I don't go to work each day." But your vocation is bigger than a job or a career, although if you have a job outside the home, that is certainly part of your vocation. Your vocation is whatever God has given you to do, wherever He has given you to do it, for the service of other people.

In the next chapter, we'll discuss the vocations each of us have in the basic unit of human society as God designed it: the family. But even beyond your calling as child, parent, spouse, and sibling, you have a vocation in the world, a place of service to the rest of mankind through the work He has given you to do, whether that happens in the nursery, the farm, an office building, or the workshop. A stay-at-home mom serves humanity quite directly by raising the next generation and training them in all aspects of life—that's her work, and quite a lot of work it is! The income-earning father serves humanity by providing for his wife and children. The farmer serves humanity by growing food. The insurance salesman serves humanity by providing a needed service and method of providing security. The janitor serves humanity by providing clean environments in which to live, study, and work. And the list goes on. All work that is not expressly sinful is significant and has a place in God's design for human society.

To find out more about vocation, read CPH's *The Spirituality of the Cross* and *The Calling: Live a Life of Significance.*

In the Beginning, Work

God created humanity to take joy and derive meaning from work. In the beginning, Adam was to work the Garden of Eden and Eve was to be a helpmeet for him in all that he did. And this happened before the fall into sin, when work gained a curse as well. But from the curses that came to Adam and Eve in their vocations, we can learn much about what the blessings of those vocations are.

> To the woman He said, "I will surely multiply your pain in childbearing; in pain you shall bring forth children. Your desire shall be for your husband, and he shall rule over you." And to Adam He said, "Because you have listened to the voice of your wife and have eaten of the tree of which I commanded you,

'You shall not eat of it,' cursed is the ground because of you; in pain you shall eat of it all the days of your life; thorns and thistles it shall bring forth for you; and you shall eat the plants of the field. By the sweat of your face you shall eat bread, till you return to the ground, for out of it you were taken; for you are dust, and to dust you shall return." The man called his wife's name Eve, because she was the mother of all living. (Genesis 3:16–20)

The first thing that comes to our attention in the curses given to Adam and Eve is the presence of conflict. If the curse is conflict between the man and the woman, then it's clear that the original blessing of Eden was for man and wife to be complementary to each other and in harmony with each other. Likewise, if the curse upon the man's work and the woman's work is "pain" (vv. 16–17), then it is clear that the original blessing of Eden for both man and woman was joy and happiness in their proper work.

Although the world is fallen and husband and wife don't always get along, we still find much joy in our marriages and strive to make them more joyful. Likewise, although the curse that humankind brought upon itself has introduced pain and hardship into our work, nevertheless, God still seeks to bless us through our work and we can still find joy in it.

Make no mistake, there is still plenty of pain and drudgery in work. God makes a special point of discussing this in that particular work which belongs to womankind alone:

giving birth to new human life. There is no "natural" event that is more painful, frightening, and dangerous, and yet this is how the joy of a new human life comes into the world.

All work shares in this combination of joy and pain, though nothing combines both extremes quite like motherhood. One of the greatest blessings you can receive in this life is work that you find fulfilling and joyful, but I guarantee that even if you love your work, it will have plenty of pain and drudgery. Likewise, if you are in a phase of your life where you are just grinding away at work that you can't stand, there will still be daily joys to be found in the work that God has given you to do.

Masks of God

So your work will have pain and it will have joy. Even the pagans probably know this much. But Christians see even more deeply into God's purpose in providing us work. Consider what Luther says in his explanation of the First Article of the Creed in the Small Catechism.

> I believe that God has made me and all creatures; that He has given me my body and soul, eyes, ears, and all my members, my reason and all my senses, and still takes care of them. He also gives me clothing and shoes, food and drink, house and home, wife and children, land, animals, and all I have. He richly and daily provides me with all that I need to support this body and life.

Did God make you, or did your parents? Did God give you clothing and shoes, or did you buy them at the store? Did God give you food and drink, or did the farmer down the road? Does God provide you all that you need to support this body and life, or do you have to work for a living and get a paycheck for those things?

Get it? God works through means, He works through the everyday ho-hum world. God provides food through farmers and truck drivers and grocery clerks. God provides new human lives through fathers and mothers. God takes care of our bodies and senses through doctors and nurses. God provides for clean communities through garbage collectors, and He provides for peace and stability through wise rulers.

So no matter what position you occupy in this world with your work, you are a "mask of God," as Luther liked to say. God is blessing the world through your work. Whether that work is small or great in the world's eyes is of little importance. The almighty and everlasting God takes great joy and pleasure in your work, and He is providing for the world through you.

Furthermore, in a greatly ironic way, God forces us to bless others through our work by making us dependent on our work. I know that I would love to spend all my time fishing, hunting, reading, and generally lying around the house. In other words, I'd love to spend my time serving myself instead of my family and the community around me. This is because I am a selfish sinner who has inherited this selfish sinfulness from my parents and ancestors all the way back to

Adam and Eve. If I were left to my own devices, I'd sit around all day doing what I thought was fun rather than doing those things that are a blessing for others.

So God has made me dependent on my work. If I don't work, I don't eat. If my wife doesn't do her work, the kids will run amok. Each of us has to find something useful to do so that we can live. And "useful" means useful to others in the community around you, because nobody will pay you for anything that isn't useful to them! So by making me dependent on my work, God has seen to it that my work will bless others.

Perspective

Do you see how such a perspective can change the way you look at the drudgery in your work? It is especially that day-in and day-out drudgery that God is using to bless others through you. Among the first people in society to embrace Christianity were the slaves in the Roman Empire. Good portions of the New Testament (1 Corinthians 7; Ephesians 6; Colossians 3; Philemon) deal with how Christian slaves should live out their lives of faith. Can you imagine anything more full of drudgery than work as a slave? Every man who is free has incomparably less drudgery and hardship in his life than a slave. Yet the most famous verse about vocation was written directly to slaves: "Whatever you do, work heartily, as for the Lord and not for men, knowing that from the Lord you will receive the inheritance as your reward. You are serving the Lord Christ" (Colossians 3:23–24).

You have been called by God to be His mask, to serve God's people by your work. Your work does not have to be "holy" or "churchly" or important and glamorous by the world's standards to be good and God-pleasing. You don't have to spend all your free time volunteering at church or for nonprofit organizations. God is already using you for His holy purposes right where you are in the work He has given you to do.

Key Points

- God has given you a vocation.

- God provides through the work of people in the world.

- Your work will bring both joys and pains.

- In your vocation, you act as a "mask of God."

Discussion Questions

1. What is your vocation? How is God using you as His "mask" through the work he has given you to do?

2. What is the joy you get from your vocation? What drudgery comes with your vocation, and how do you push through it?

3. How will living a Jesus-centered life by setting aside time for church, Bible reading, and prayer make you stronger in your vocation?

Action Steps

1. Pray with your vocation in mind that God would bless others through your work. Give thanks to God for the vocations of others.

2. Make a point of talking about your current job as part of your God-given vocation, and encourage other Christians to do so as well.

Before God gave you any other vocation,

He called you to be a son or a daughter. He called you into a family. Then He called you into His family in Baptism. Since then, maybe He's called you to be a husband or wife, mom or dad, sister or brother or only child, an orphan or widow, or a grandpa or grandma. These are our primary vocations, and at the end of the day, these are what matter most. Our work in the vocations that God gives us "out there" are important, and God uses them to serve humanity, but we serve humanity most directly by serving that part of humanity God has called us into closest proximity with: our family. To put it another way, God calls us to love our neighbors as ourselves, and there is no set of neighbors closer to us than our family.

Yet is there anyone harder to love than your family? Isn't it easier to be kinder to a stranger than to your own flesh and blood? Indeed, I see more people in my office about family problems than any other kind, and I would bet any other pastor sees the same.

There's no easy solution to this problem. It's hardest to act like a true Christian, a truly Jesus-centered person, with the people who see you all the time. You can't hide from your family like you can from people out in the world precisely because the masks we put on for the rest of the world make us tired. It's hard pretending to be patient and kind. It wears us out, and so our family bears the brunt of our real personalities with all our impatience and anger.

It's always been this way, well, ever since that curse on our family relationships fell on Adam and Eve, as we saw in the last chapter. There is no easy solution other than a life of continual repentance and faith. But I do believe that the world today is encroaching on the Christian home as never before. The world wants more of your time, more of you, and more of your family.

Make Time

You hear a lot of poignant things from people on their deathbeds—and a lot of sad things, a lot of regrets. But here are three things that I've never heard from somebody on his or her deathbed: I wish I had spent more time at work; I wish we'd had fewer kids; I wish I knew what my bank balance is right now. The deathbed gives perspective; blessed are those who can gain the perspective without having to wait for the deathbed.

Remember that your life is nothing more than a collection of time. Consider your weekly schedule when it comes to the time you spend with your family. Are you making the time to be the father or mother God wants you to be? Do you spend time teaching your kids to pray and read the Word of God? Do you and your spouse have a strong relationship, or do you hardly talk to each other anymore? Do you know what the great fears and hopes of your children, your parents, your siblings, and your friends are? Do they know yours? Do you spend more time handling your Facebook friends than your flesh-and-blood family?

Don't wait for tomorrow to make the time for this family space in your life. Habits are hard to break, and they only get harder the longer you wait.

In a way it's difficult to write this chapter and still make it apply to anyone and everyone who might read it. Not everybody has kids, not everybody is married, not everybody has the same family situation. But no matter what your situation is, making progress in living out a Jesus-centered life with your family really will come down to time. It takes time to build relationships with people, time specifically dedicated to that task.

Key Points

- Our primary vocations are our family relationships.

- The family is under attack by the world, the flesh, and the devil.

- Families must spend time together to be strong and lasting.

- You must be intentional about setting aside time to fulfill your family vocation.

Discussion Questions

1. What do you think your parents/spouse/children would say is the thing you do best in your vocation as their family member? The thing you do least well?

2. How many nights a week do you actually spend together as a family?

3. What are some of your favorite memories about your parents and siblings from growing up? Do you notice anything about those memories that might help you in your family vocation now?

Action Steps

1. Set aside time to conduct family devotions—a short period of Bible reading and prayer—each day.

2. Eat the evening meal together as a family every night (or at least set a goal of X number of nights per week to get started).

3. Go down to one TV, and even consider giving that up as a family in Lent, on Sundays, or for some other short period of time.

4. Start with one night of the week that is reserved to spend time together as a family playing a game, going for a walk, or some other group activity.

If you do these five things—go to church, go read, go pray, go work, and come home—your Christian life will be deepened. That deepening won't happen because of your works; it will happen because what I am encouraging you to do is to leave your self-made works aside and get more of Jesus' Word and Sacraments into your life. Living a Jesus-centered life is just that easy, and it's just that hard. Seize the gifts Christ has given you and see if you are not blessed in them. Do not for a moment think that anything other than Jesus' Word and gifts in Baptism, Absolution, and the Lord's Supper could ever be a key to spiritual strength. Our strength is Christ. Our justification, life, and salvation are in Christ. Our only hope is connecting to Him through the means He has given us.

As I sit in my office tidying up the conclusion to this manuscript, it happens to be Ash Wednesday, the beginning of the great penitential season of Lent. These forty-odd days are the Church's call to all of us to slow down and refresh our Christian life. Most churches offer extra church services during this time of year, and the discipline of fasting, prayer, and almsgiving is encouraged. It's an active season in the Church's life where we are reminded and motivated to reconnect to our Christian faith and live it out.

Yet the words that go with the ashes for which Ash Wednesday is named are these: "For you are dust, and to dust you shall return" (Genesis 3:19). The words spoken to Adam are spoken to us. As we stand on the edge of Lent, we are returned to the edge of the Garden of Eden and are cast out.

That's the perfect introduction to the Christian life for Christians who are serious about deepening their faith. You are dust. The strength is not in you. If you lean on your own resources, you will fail. Your sinfulness means that you are headed back to dust.

So cling to the One who took up Adam's dusty flesh, who went down into the dusty tomb hewn out of the rock by sin, and yet who rose again. Cling to Jesus. Come learn from Him in church and receive Him in the Sacrament. Come hear His living voice in Absolution. Go read His Word and be filled with His wisdom. Pour out your heart to Him in prayer and be formed by prayers from His Word; then take that Word, and therefore Him, with you into your calling and bring Him back home to your family. Our life is Christ—our Jesus-centered life—it's truly that simple.